Grandma's Memoirs

Gladys Kennedy

1927 - 2021

*The Journal of a Pioneer's Daughter,
Composed in her Later Years*

Copyright Notice

© Gladys Kennedy & Michael Raymond Astle 2022

Except as provided by the Copyright Act 1968 (Australia), no part of this publication may be reproduced and/or communicated to the public without the prior written permission of the publisher.

All Rights Reserved

ISBNs:	978-0-9941799-9-9 (print)
	978-1-922758-99-6 (digital)
Publication year:	2022
Book Title:	Grandma's Memoirs: The Journal of a Pioneer's Daughter, Composed in her Later Years
Original Working Title:	Mum's Journal: A Collection of true stories from the past.
Language:	English
Publisher:	Michael Raymond Astle
Printer:	Ingram Spark
Location:	Melbourne, Australia
Author:	Gladys Kennedy (nee Stennett)
Editor:	Michael Raymond Astle
Binding:	Paperback - Perfect Bound
Target Audience:	Family
Subjects:	LCO015000 LITERARY COLLECTIONS / Diaries & Journals
	HIS004000 HISTORY / Australia & New Zealand
	LCO005000 LITERARY COLLECTIONS / Australian & Oceanian
Regional Subject:	6.0.1.0.2.0.0 New South Wales
	1MBF-AU-N New South Wales
Thema Subjects:	DND Diaries, letters & journals
	NHM Australasian & Pacific history
Qualifiers:	2ACBM Australian English
	3MP 20th century

Contents

Introduction..4
Mum's Journal..5
Comboyne...6
The "Hot Cat"...7
The Hat...8
The Scooter..9
School days..10
Picnics Prospect Dam..11
The old House at Comboyne..12
Work at Comboyne...13
Neighbors...14
Learning to drive..15
Early years at Toongabbie...16
Memories...17
More Neighbors...18
More Neighbors...19
More Childhood Memories..20
Growing Up..21
The garden...22
Two Sides to a neighbour..23
New Home...24
Cats I've had..25
The Villa..26
Hopewood House...27
Brothers...28
1930's Depression Years..29
1930's..30
My Villa...31
Still on 2012..32
Still in hospital 2012...33
(Untitled)...34
Health..35
Xmas 2013..36
Marriages..37
(Untitled)...38
Extra Stories..39
My first day at Chatham Primary School..40
Walking to hospital standing all day ironing then walk home when boys were young..41
Index of Pictures...42
Epilogue..43

Introduction

It's been a few years now since Grandma gave me her notebook headed "Mum's Journal" with the intent that I should publish it. In the mean time, I've collected some family photographs to fill up the pages. Not every picture relates to the story on the same page as itself but I hope they at least give some impression of the era Grandma reflects upon throughout much of her writing.

In regards to editing, I have taken a minimalist approach. Even my choice of font is intended to be similar to Grandma's style of handwriting. While minor scribal errors have been corrected, archaic and alternative spellings reflective of the era have been retained. Likewise, phrasings representative of Grandma's manner of speech have been preserved.

I have, however, added numerous footnotes throughout the work in my own voice. These are primarily intended to assist those unfamiliar with our family history to understand what Grandma means. As with all families, there may well be different views about certain matters held by others. This could well be said of other people mentioned in the text too. As such, I must beg the pardon of anyone who may take exception to any of the assertions made either in the text or in my footnotes, or both. For my own part, I'm only trying to convey what I've heard as best I can recall it.

In 2020, Grandma celebrated her 93rd birthday with my father and step-mum visiting while still residing in Taree, as she had for over half a century. Only, she no longer left the hostel. The restrictions of later that year prevented this book's sooner publication. Sadly, Grandma passed away the following year.

Mum's Journal
by
Gladys Kennedy (nee Stennett)

A Collection of true stories from the past.

It started at "Waterfalls" Comboyne where I was born on 5th February 1927. My father died a few months later so I never knew him.

Mum took us girls to the city where Grandfather Hutchby built us a house at Toongabbie, where we lived untill I was 14. I later found out it had to be sold to save the estate farm on Comboyne. We all got a small amount, 300 pounds when I turned 21. Brother Bob bought the farm in a run down condition & built it up into a first class property.

I remained close to sister May all her life as she more or less brought me up; even when she married I spent a lot of holidays with her & Glen.

I found out many years later, when Dad died Mum handed me to May saying she didn't want me.[1]

---

[1] Grandma was the youngest of around 13 children. (The exact number I've been told over the years seems to vary slightly, probably because a few of the children died in infancy.) With her father John dying right before the Great Depression began, her mother simply couldn't cope with another baby at that time.

Comboyne.

Bob used to grow potatoes and employed workers. Once when Bess & I were about 12 we holidayed at the farm.[2] One old chap "Mundy Grean" had a horse which he used to ride bare-back, just a sugar bag & reins, another had a bicycle, which we had a loan of to ride to town some 5 miles away. I rode the horse; no matter how I tried it would only jog. Here we were in town & down to the butter factory, when all of a sudden the horse starting rearing up & me shrieking & Bess laughing. But I hung on knowing locals were waiting to see a city girl fall off. After awhile we made it back to the farm. No way would Bess swap me the bike.
Boy did I have a sore rear-end. When we told the old chap.[3] When we told the old chap what happened, in a drawling voice said, "I meant to tell you not to go near the factory, he don't like the noise.

---
[2] Bob was ten years older than Grandma.
[3] It's likely Grandma paused here to laugh at the memory before continuing, hence the repetition.

The "Hot Cat".

Now Bob had a black cat who on cold nights liked nothing better than to sleep near or even on the stove when we had all gone to bed. The oven door would be left open to warm the house.

Bob's habit of a morning was to light the stove, then over to dairy to get it ready for milking, then back to the house for a cup of tea & something to eat. (This is before he married Jean.)

Hearing a noise in oven he opened the door & poor puss who had been asleep there all night flew out & disappeared for nearly a week. He didn't go near that stove again.

Bob had some draught horses. He used to hook them up to a slide, a solid piece of wood connected to the horses by chains. Away we would go down to the back paddock sitting on this slide & come home laden with pumkins, squash, watermelons. What a rough ride but Bess & I loved it.

The Hat.

One time Bess & I were returning to Sydney from a holiday at Comboyne.

We were in a dog-box carriage, a small separate carriage. Bess wore a lovely black picture hat which she wore with pride. Along came a gust of wind and away went the hat. It landed in a paddock of cows. It really was funny but Bess didn't think so.

Bess lived opposite us at Toongabbie. Her sister Jean later married brother Bob. We used to make our own fun as toys and money was scarce.

The fun we had with a rope tied to the lid of a drum. We used to pull each other down a steep slope.

Needless to say our underwear suffered as a result, torn & tattered. Many a hiding I received but the fun was worth it. I taught Jean to ride a bike when she started work. She was going good too untill she turned around and saw I wasn't holding the seat and promply fell off.

The Scooter

One of the neighbors boy had a scooter, this was a real old one. No tyres no brake & no wood to stand on, just the iron frame.

Well away we would go down the steep hills (and there were many) full pelt.

When I think back now it is a miracle we didn't kill ourselves. We all had a ton of fun.

Mum had a big black dog and I vividly remember the bread & pie man calling and Darky charged. Pies & bread went everywhere of-course. Mum had to buy them. I think we salvaged most as we were hungry & couldn't waste them.

We had a lot of fruit trees. As soon as it looked a bit ripe we ate it. Especially the loquats dipping them in salt, ah they were tasty. One time Mum caught us & the whip was out. Bess went home screaming that Mrs Stennett was killing Doris[4] & Gladys. However we survived but never forgot.

Doris & me.

---

[4] Doris was the sister closest to Grandma in age but their personalities often disagreed. After May died aged 89 and they were the only two siblings left, they became friendly until Doris suddenly died too after a prick from a rose thorn led to blood poisoning.

School days

We used to walk about 2 miles to school across a lot of paddocks. One time Mrs Best had an old Billy Goat & he got out & chased us head down & charging. Boy did we move. Only just made it over a fence with Billy goat & Mrs Best behind running.

We had a lot of large peppercorn trees in the school yard and our favorite game was to hang by the knees from branches to see who could hang the longest.

The headmaster caught me (everyone else had disappeared) and I had to stand in front of class as an exhibition of a monkey.

I loved school & won a bursary aged 11.[5] But Mum wouldn't let me go on as none of the others had.[6] Edna & May offered to buy the uniforms too. So there I stayed in 6th class till I was 14 and then it was rotten factory work. It made me determined that if I ever had children they would be educated to the best of their ability.

Doris & me

---

[5] Grandma actually won a bursary three years in a row.
[6] What Grandma surprisingly leaves out here (considering how often she would talk about it) is that it was her well-built sister Doris who protested that none of the other siblings received a high school education. Grandma believed she was jealous and used her stature to intimidate their mother into preventing her from receiving the opportunity. This was a cause of lasting tension throughout their lives.

Picnics Prospect Dam.

Nearly every Sunday our outing was a walk of some miles to Prospect Dam[7] and have a picnic.

There was a chain swing in the back yard, had fun on it untill May fell off & broke her collar-bone. So it was banned but we got around that.

For some reason, every Sunday morning out would come the Senna tea, to clean out our bowels. It is vile. Doris used to drink hers outside & of-course tip it out. But as I was smaller & didn't threaten mum, had to drink in front of her. How we didn't get ill or even die with all the green fruit & wild berries we used to eat I'll never know.

Glen[8] (May's husband) said we had cast iron stomachs. Often stayed with May & Glen; she had a pet magpie. Now the toilet was in the back yard and the wretched bird would wait untill one was in there to threaten us. One would scream for May to remove him otherwise our legs would be bleeding from his beck.[9]

---

[7] Prospect Dam is in Western Sydney. Obviously this refers to the time when the family was living there.
[8] Glen was the uncle of Bob Carr who became the Premier of New South Wales some years later.
[9] Grandma's notes clearly read "beck" however I suspect she meant either "beak" or "peck" but it is impossible to tell which.

The old House at Comboyne

When my sons were young we shared a house at Comboyne with Thelma Hardy & son & daughter. Thelma was on treatment for nerves but was very good to me.

Talk about old the house was almost falling down. Sections of floor boards were missing. The Bathroom was in such a state it couldn't be used. No laundry. We used to boil clothes outside in a kerosene tin and wash in a small plastic bowl (which I still have under the laundry tub).[10] It is a reminder of harder times. The outside toilet was a sight, pan type, and almost falling down.

The first night there the three of us[11] huddled together as rats ran around the ceiling. I bought ratsak next day.

The old fuel stove shelves were proped up with jam tins. I cooked mostly on a small metho stove.

None the less we survived for about 18 months untill we got a commission home in Taree. We stayed there for some years untill I formed another bad relationship with a very jealous man[12] who didn't treat my boys well so again we were off on our own. Still, we made lots of friends and when we were given an even better commission house I bought with encouragement from Clive and here we stayed. I worked and saved to pay for it[13] and so no one could be prouder.

---

[10] Grandma wrote this while she was residing in the house she bought from the Housing Commission near the showground in Taree.

[11] The "three of us" refers to Grandma and her two sons after she left their father. While it is difficult to be sure so many years later, he may have been suffering from undiagnosed "shell shock", as it later became known, as a result of his war service. (The condition is now more commonly known as Post-Traumatic Stress Disorder.) Whatever the case, his inability to hold down a job was a bane to Grandma and she considered him an unsuitable example for the boys. Nonetheless, she remained in contact with her father-in-law all his own life.

[12] The original text reads "zealous" however Grandma's second husband was violent and she used to regularly describe him as jealous so this has been changed as a probable slip of the pen.

[13] The year her union obtained equal pay for women, her son Clive (my father) suggested she use the extra to purchase the house. While it was good fortune for her, Grandma had voted against equal pay for fear the Speedo

Work at Comboyne

I worked mostly picking potatoes, corn, peas, whatever was going.
Brother Bob kept us in vegies.
I worked at the bread shop for over a year. The baker was a nice man but his wife was horrible to me. Wash & polish every room every-day besides cooking meals & looking after the shop. One incident stands out in my mind. Clive had his tonsils out at Wauchope. Albert took me down with him after work. Next day I asked to able to go & see him. She refused saying if I went my job went too.
As I had no income other than what I earned, I couldn't go. It was heart-breaking.
Next thing she sacked me and put a young girl on at less money. I had the last laugh as the girl got pregnant and left. In Taree I did house-work untill I got work in the hospital laundry. As we had no car I had to walk to the hospital,[14] stand all day pressing uniforms then walk home.

factory would move offshore to a country with lower wages if the motion passed. Grandma's fears were well founded as it did just that shortly after she retired.

[14] It was about a 5 km walk to the hospital.

Neighbors

Mostly I had good neighbors but one was an exception. She was there nearly 4 years before being evicted.

Heather was one of life's misfits. There was Austar[15] on the roof, cigarette in hand, mobile phone[16] on hip and she couldn't pay the light bill.[17] Power was off more times than it was on. There at one time was two large bull terrier dogs. One had 12 pups in a bedroom & the cat had six kittens inside as well. After some time I noticed one dog was missing. She calmly said, oh we came home one day and it was dead in the lounge room after eating the foam stuffing out of the lounge! Then the cats went missing, the dogs had ate them! So away went the remaining dogs & new ones came. Not as savage thank goodness. The things I saw out my kitchen window.[18] They had bricks supporting a sheet of tin and did cooking on it. I was too frightened to go to bed in case of house fire. Flames reached the gutter of the house. Candles flickering inside curtains black & torn, flyscreens hanging off windows & broken windows. They had one bedroom turned into an aviary, 5 large green parrotts. When she left they had ate all the woodwork & stink the house & carpet smelt of urine. It will cost thousands to repair.[19] She lost the front door key one time so a lounge window was left open and they all crawled in including dogs.

How the other half lives

---

[15] This was a brand of satellite television which was expensive in the 1990's.

[16] While the cost of a mobile phone began to reduce in the later part of the decade, at this time it was still considered an unnecessary luxury except for businessmen.

[17] Grandma always referred to the electricity bill as the "light bill" as that had originally been the primary purpose of household electricity of which she could remember the early days.

[18] Grandma's kitchen window was positioned above the sink where it just so happened to look out over her neighbour's back yard due to the slope of the land and Grandma's house being on stilts.

[19] Grandma is relating her own thought at the time in this sentence, hence the tense.

Learning to drive

I got my licence in 1954 and decided to give it up in 2004.[20] It was quite an art in those days with gears, no signals on cars; it was all done by hand signals from the driver, and changing gears whilst keeping eyes on the road.

I was staying at sister May's at Duri near Tamworth. Glen took me in his old 1927 chev,[21] with hand throttle on steering wheel.

Half-way to Werris Creek, the Ute stopped. Glen had to lift the bonnett & turn the petrol on. I kept my licence current until I bought my first car, a Volkswagen. Since then I bought a new 180B Datsun after I had been working some years at Speedo. Then a second hand Sigma automatic sedan.

Nowadays I catch a bus and community bus give me half price taxi vouchers and neighbor aid have day trips which are enjoyable. I don't see family as much as I'd like as they live far-away but with phone calls we keep in touch and have visits often. I go to Bingo once a week and cards once a week. The rest of the time is spent gardening, reading, and trying to play the piano.[22]

---

[20] Grandma surrendered her licence of her own accord once she felt as though her reaction time was not as swift as it used to be. Her doctor at the time encouraged her that there was no need to yet but she had determined that she was ready.

[21] i.e. Chevrolet (a brand of motor vehicle)

[22] Grandma was actually very good at the piano but she always felt as though she could have been much better. After her mother had sold their family's pianola, Grandma was unable to continuing learning. Whenever she related the story in later years, she would always add, "... and I was just starting to learn how to play the popular music." An example of this is seen in another story later in this work.

Early years at Toongabbie

It was a lovely weatherboard house my grandfather had built.

Mum was a good gardener; we had lots of fruit trees.

Needless to say a lot of fruit was eaten green.

Bread was delivered by horse & cart, also meat & ice for the ice box, no fridge, we only had to shop for groceries.

I remember the old Tivolia[23] building in Sydney where we sometimes went to see stage shows. It was a big place & we had to sit in the cheap seats called in the God's, it was up in the high part of the roof, and the people looked as small as ants on the stage. It was an outing we enjoyed.

We had had lovely Sunday school picnics in Parramatta Park, lots of goodies and races.

We had a large kitchen table and used a net & sm.[24] bats to play table tennis; it was a good pastime.

Mum also had a pianola which I loved and would have liked to buy it off her when she decided to sell in my teens but wouldn't let me and I was learning music too. After we moved to a smaller house which in turn we had to move to ½ house (called a flat) which I hated.

Mum May Edna Doris & me

---

[23] Although I have retained Grandma's original spelling, I highly suspect she means the old Tivoli Theatre.

[24] This is probably Grandma's shorthand for "small" but just in case she meant "some", it seemed best to let the reader decide which is more likely.

Memories.

I had some lovely breaks with Aunty Eva who had a senior policeman husband. She made me my first dress. I loved it as all I had ever had was hand me downs. I also stayed with Aunty Lil at Bondi. She lived upstairs with trams rattling past all the time, and of-course with May & Glen who constantly fed me cod-liver oil, I can still taste the horrible stuff, as I was a skinny weed. It didn't fatten me up.
Then there was Grandma & Grandad (Mum's parents). I loved being with them as I felt loved and happy.
One time when they lived at Hurstville we went to the beach at Sans Souci. We collected a bucket of pippies to eat. Came home put them in a pot then Grandma looked at me and said "I don't fancy eating them do you?" I certainly didn't so they were thrown out. When Grandad died Grandma came to live with us. She was lovely. But then Aunt Lil came and took her, as she thought she left money, but there was none as Grandad had lost his houses. I don't know the story. I remember they were purple brick homes in Forest Rd, Hurstville; he was a builder.

More Neighbors

The next to come was single mother two teenage boys. Mum as usual sat and watched T.V. all day but the boys did work at Wingham abattoirs. But when they suddenly disappeared, and a commission again came to clean up, what a mess. Then debt collectors called on me to ask their new address. They owed money everywhere. I couldn't help as I didn't know.

At the present time a single mum with three young ones 1, 2, 3 in age, watched video all day, the kiddies, played in yard in plastic nappies unsupervised. Always wanting to borrow till I put a stop to it after seeing car load of visitors stay and drink all night loud music nearly drive me mad, then want to borrow things. I told her to look after her family not entertain people. Anyhow she was evicted and the sheriff called on me for her whereabouts. She owed money as well.

The cleaners were in to-day and used a rake to clean inside. I went in to talk to see who was coming in. It is sold but the agent Hooker is handling things not the housing commission. So here hoping. The laundry & near-pantry was piled high with dirty clothes & nappies. Two trucks' loads taken away. Filthy woman.

More Neighbors.

At last the house next door is sold and the owner is living there.

What a difference. She has been working non-stop, cleaning, painting and new carpet, new fencing and the garden is starting to look like someone lives there. She is very good to me helps a lot.

I happened to mention I wish the edging on my porch garden was higher. No trouble, off we go to Brickworks & cement at Bunnings. I went inside in the mean-time Anna had finished the edging as good a job as any man could have done, a froget[25] she called it. She has a lovely big dog and a talking parrott.

Also I was unfortunate to have what appeared to be a boil on my back. I couldn't even see it. But Anna dressed it for me every-day. I ended up at the doctors & had it lanced. It was an abscess. We go to Old Bar beach early of a Sunday morning & walk on the beach. She is a lot younger than me but we get along fine. Has 3 grown up daughters living in Sydney. She is a good house painter so I've paid her to do some for me. And a very good job too.

---
[25] This word is unfamiliar to anyone I've asked about it. Perhaps it may be jargon or a neologism.

More Childhood Memories

There was an orchard behind us at Toongabbie. One afternoon Bess & I decided we would like some oranges. We crawled under the barbed wire fence & had some rolled up in our frocks. Next thing a rifle shot & yelling! Boy did we move but we didn't drop our loot. Hiding under bushes next to the house we stayed untill after dark, too terrified to go home. Our one and only crime.

We went to the beach once. To save changing, wore our costumes under dresses. As mum hadn't packed undies we came home minus any.

May & Glen & young family lived with us for awhile in Toongabbie to help mum. But we still lost the house. I did miss all my friends.

We lived at Parramatta for some years but mum decided the house was too big and we moved and of all things she sold our piano and I was learning popular music, but mum only thought of herself. The next house we had to get out and ended up in two rooms (called a flat) at Harbord.[26] It was awfull, no privacy at all. I had to share a room with mum. We had no bathroom or laundry. I realise now I should have got a flat with girl friends, but felt I had to stay with mum.

---

[26] This suburb's name has since been changed to Freshwater.

Growing Up

It wasn't easy making new friends. After working in Bonds factory for some years I moved to their underwear machines in Sydney. Once Manpower was over (after War 2) we all shifted to better work rooms. I loved it at Chic Salon, making beautifull underwear. I made some nice friends there.

Met various boys but I was naive. Mum didn't tell me anything only if I gat pregnant not to come home. I was too scared to even kiss a boy.

As I grew up I found out the hard way once I married. Everything was in his name all though I was the one working to pay bills. I was told he married me cause I was a good worker, and he had grand ideas which changed all the time.[27]

I pestered him to at least build a house as I wanted children and I had found out the law said I couldn't get a divorce. The law changed and I did after waiting 5 years.[28] But I got nothing as he owned it all. My neighbors Anne & Eric were wonderfull to me and stood by me as friends for many years untill they died. I worked on a machine at home (factory cut out) even right up untill I went into labour. He said I wanted the house so I could pay for it. So I left and came to Comboyne. Bob[29] helped a lot & we eventually got a commission home at Taree.

---

[27] Grandma's first husband (my grandfather) was without any regular income.

[28] The number '5' is in blue in the original but the surrounding text is black, indicating that Grandma added this in later. However, with the exception of cases of adultery, it is correct that when divorce laws were introduced in Australia a couple had to have been estranged for 5 years before either party could file for it.

The garden

I get great pleasure out of gardening. In the back yard I have a bird bath next to it is a grevillea which birds are attracted to. Every morning as I have my break-fast, I watch the passing parade of birds. First come the magpie family which now includes a young one. They have a great old time and manage to empty the bath. The pee-wees next and don't they make a noise to let me know it is empty of water. I refill & enjoy. They are bossy birds. The poor doves sit & wait. In the meantime rainbow lorikeet parrots are in the grevillea tree, such pretty birds.

Also is a large tree which with the help of grandson Michael we placed native rock lily orchids in the fork, what a display when they bloom.

Near-by is a laden orange tree, against the fence is a paw-paw tree which I grew from seed; it also has a good crop.

The front garden is a picture with colorfull shrubs & flowers and bulb in season. In the fernery is a magnificent staghorn; its fronds reaching to the ground. Maiden hair fern covers the ground & the canopy is a orange bell creeper. You can imagine what it looks like in flower.

---

[29] Grandma's brother who bought the family farm, to the ire of at least one elder brother who believed the right to redeem it was his own.

Two Sides to a neighbour[30]

After being a nice neighbor Anna changed. She stormed in one day and asked for her key back. No explanation. I was puzzled and as I knew her birthday was soon I bought a really nice card and rang her to sing happy birthday only to have the phone slammed down on me. She then went out. I waited for her to come home so I knocked on her door and asked what was wrong. Boy did she explode, shouting & screaming abuse at me saying how I gave her a lousy card and no present and also I was spying on her. My windows look over her side so I can't help but look.[31] She was totally out of control it frightened me. I just looked on in amazement & came home. She hasn't spoke since. Since a wall of sorts has come up. It is so silly. She is like two people. Any how I've since put my house on the market & hope to move into a unit in a retirement village. So far on sale. I hope it won't be long.[32] I really want peace & quiet.

---

[30] It is hard to know exactly what the truth surrounding this story might be. The incident described occurred around the time Grandma's memory began to slip. It's possible she may have said or done something to cause offence without either realising or remembering it. I do recall my father communicating with Anna to try and bring some peace to the matter but I don't know how successful his efforts may have been.

[31] Grandma's kitchen window was positioned above the sink where it just so happened to look out over her neighbour's back yard due to the slope of the land and Grandma's house being on stilts.

[32] Although Grandma was initially reluctant to sell the house she had worked to fully own, she soon decided she would be better off selling.

New Home

After 5 months the house was finally sold, as I had put a deposit on a villa in a retirement village. It was moving day. Clive & Rohaini[33] came down and stayed a week with me and helped me move. We had the keys on the Wed and boy did they work. Emptied all cupboards and wardrobes, and drove back and forth all day. Piled everything in the bathroom even laundry. So all the carriers had to bring was the empty furniture. What a saving. I gave Clive $100 for petrol, worth much more. I had change to buy a set top box & hands free phone, a door bell which plays a tune.
I was so gratefull to them both.
I have settled in, done a little gardening but one bed is clay. It was like digging concrete. Have to get something to break it up. Have lovely neighbor, have known her many years. Played bowls[34] together and play cards at church hall every Wed. It is a lovely brick 2 bed villa. I can now relax & enjoy life. Now I am enjoying getting a garden ready. I do love flowers and a garden gives so much pleasure.

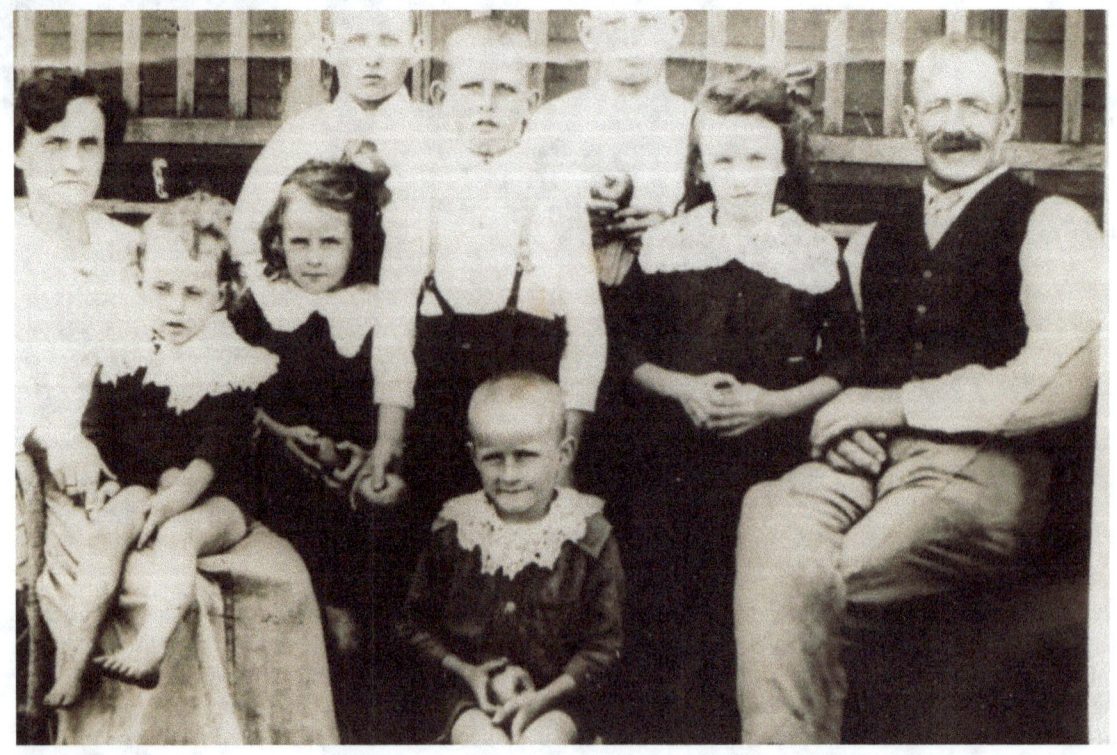

---
[33] My father and step-mum.
[34] Grandma was a champion indoor (carpet) bowls player.

Cats I've had.

Rufus was a large tom. Boss of everything. When I used to leave for work of a morning he would stroll next door and spend the day there but when they were away I had to feed their cat. Rufus would put on a performance & chase her away so he would be locked inside glaring through the glass. I remember one incident a young dog came into the yard where a certain cat was sleeping. Next thing, screams from a howling dog as Rufus rode him like a jockey up the street. He never came back for a repeat performance. Also the Alsatians from across the road would always by-pass our house & cat.

We had him 18 years.

Next was Tigger, a ginger tom. I then decided not to have another as I was getting old. But I still have a soft spot for cats.

The Villa

Been here 3 months now and the maintenance man has put up lovely new curtain tracks and fire-proof rubber back curtains at no cost to me. In the new year I hope to get the factory out to get some dress curtains. It is Xmas now. I had lunch out with my friend of many years Margaret Moran.[35] My small garden is looking good. The gardener replaced the gravel and plastic with lovely soil. Kay[36] gave me a gardenia shrub which has big white flowers in bloom. I also have a sm.[37] garden with lattice all planted with some reminders of my big garden. Also lots of pot plants.

We have a library and hairdresser at Bushland Place[38] which I use.

Still get up early, have breakfast and go for a walk.

No more stress and worry. A lot of magpies here, they are making short work of my outside mats.

All security screens on all windows & doors, also locks. At night sensor lights all around, and call button if needed, and regular bus service.

[39] I now have my dress curtains, lovely cream flowers on cream sheer & scalloped hem. Just valances in kitchen & lounge as I like to read and have doors open for light & air.

---

[35] Margaret worked at the hospital laundry with Grandma.
[36] Grandma's niece (daughter of Bob) who was the last of the Stennett family to remain on Comboyne, although her name had changed with marriage.
[37] This is probably Grandma's shorthand for "small".
[38] Although they were located on different sites, this is the name of nursing home which ran the retirement village and so they offered access to some of their services to the residents of both.
[39] The final paragraph of this page was penned in blue, suggesting a later addition.

Hopewood House.

When I worked at Chick Salon making lovely underwear, the owner S. O. Bailey had a house at Bowral, Hopewood House, for unmarried mothers in 1940's. Selected girls could spend the weekend there free of cost but helping out. My friend Joan & I spent many a weekend, looking after babies & children; he kept them untill 18 years of age. It was wonderfull.

Joan & I also found work at Cahills restaurant[40] in Sydney. We caught a tram after work no tea straight to Cahill's to waitress, the chefs were good. If the supervisor was not looking we had a feed. We did that for some months, as wages were low. I would have loved to improve things but it wasn't free like it is now.

[41]When we lived at Plummer St.[42] while I was at work one day Trevor[43] played with a bow & arrow and it resulted in a large hole in the wall. He was only young but immediately raced off to get plaster & fixed it up & I never found out untill years later, so good was his work. I also have a wooden step-ladder he made at school; used it lots of times when I made curtains at home.

---

[40] Cahills Restaurants of Distinction were advertised as being "where the standard of food and service is consistently high." Grandma used this opportunity to learn about table etiquette.
[41] The final paragraph of this page was penned in blue, suggesting another later addition.
[42] Grandma's first commission house in Taree
[43] Grandma's elder son, my uncle

Brothers.

After dad died my brothers wanted to be on the farm but apparently mum refused so they went bush with crosscut saws & axe. While working one day my elder brother Harry was killed by a falling limb, he was only 19. I was still only very young so I don't remember him. So I bought many years later the grave plot next to dad & Harry on Comboyne. It is all paid for, funeral and all.

Jack was pilot(?) for years then settled on a property at Pappinbarra out of Wauchope. It was isolated but lovely rain forest & he grew & sold all native plants, even had tourists there.

Bill had a farm at Warrell Creek & grew bananas as well. Bees also. Later he retired to Nambucca Heads.

Albert had a farm at Comboyne after being in the air-force for some years and of course Bob finally bought the farm which he made a success of.

I spent many happy holidays there & he was a big help to me in later years when I was on my own.

His daughter Kay is very good. I often see her and she helps me gardening, gave me a lovely gardenia shrub. I gave her a lot of things from my place before I sold it.

1930's Depression Years.

I was only very young but well remember them. We didn't have much money and grew most vegies, us children helping. I can distinctly remember mum cooking tripe which is only tolerable in the best of cooks but done with water and no butter. I'll leave it to your imagination. Naturally we didn't like but in those days it did not matter; you didn't eat it one meal it was served up the next. So being hungry it was eaten, then outside we would go & pinch whatever fruit was nearly ripe in the orchard. It is a wonder we didn't get sick, the bush things we ate, but if you are hungry it does not matter. Times were tough but we all survived and rarely got sick. I feel I'm in luxury now on a pension and don't have to work for it.

Albert and his mate Lew Davies[44] used to go out at night and next morning in bags there would be water melons, fruit & things. I realise now that they robbed orchards but then we just loved them.

They also had ferretts, horrible things, and went rabbit hunting.

---

[44] Grandma's handwriting is unclear here so I've guessed this man's name based upon what I can decipher and the style of names prevalent in that era.

1930's

Now Lew & Albert had old motorbikes, no mufflers, tearing round the district, eventually they had to quieten them or else. Did I say Albert was a boxer under the name Tiger Stennett? Bess and I used to hide behind a fruit tree & watch them till they caught us. It was fun. Anything amused us in those days.

Bess & Jean's father was a returned man from the 1918 war[45] & had one leg as did the taxi driver. They used to go to the races on Saturdays and entertain us all at midnight drunk and singing Scottish songs on their front lawn. There were no neighbors only us opposite.

Their poor mother was ruled with a rod of iron. If she went shopping to Parramatta and missed a train home she would walk[46] miles home as the dinner had to be on the table when he wanted it. I can still see her. I think Bess bought her some new clothes when he died and took her to pictures for the first time. They didn't even have electricity.

---

[45] i.e. World War I
[46] The word "walk" is missing from the original but seems obvious to supply.

My Villa

In 2012, I went to Foster shopping on the community bus. Had a lovely day. I had an experience I'll never forget. As I walked to the bus to come home I unfortunately tripped over a barrier and broke bones in my fingers & hand. The driver took me to a nurse who called an ambulance. So in I get and took to Taree hospital which confirmed the break. The aged care nurses descended on me like locusts. Couldn't set my hand for a week as it was swollen but firmly bandaged it. Then had plaster up to my elbow. Talk about traumatic. Nurses came every day to shower and check on me. I felt so helpless as I had hit my head as well. Thought I'd had some sort of a turn but I know I didn't. Even the social worker came and insisted I needed, my will needed an alteration to cover me.[47] I'm so grateful Clive agreed & I had to fill in my wishes & the solicitor came to my unit. Even had a male nurse[48] who was lovely.

When I eventually went out, I discovered one of my fellow bingo players had a bad turn in her car. When police were called she didn't know who she was and after hospital she went into a nursing home. It so upset me. I'm now looking after myself but the hand aches a lot. My 85th birthday was the next day.

---
[47] Technically, this was when Grandma arranged for power of attorney rather than an alteration to her will.
[48] The nursing profession was dominated by women at that time.

Still on 2012.

I visited Clive for Michael passed his Master degree in Religious Studies. I was so proud. He is studying more to get a better pass.[49]

Once home I was in pain with sciatica. The panadol was not strong enough. So as my Dr. was away another one in the practice gave me stronger ones, but he didn't tell me to only take one at night. I ended up falling over. What a mess. I was black & blue all over. They ended up putting me in care at the hostel for 2 weeks. I'm home now but it stripped all my confidence. But I'm getting better.

Yesterday I had a growth taken off my foot, stitches out next week so hopefully no more troubles and I can get back to outings again.

It is 2 years since I moved and I'm happy. When the stitches came out, blood shot everywhere. I had a bad infection. On strong antibiotics it took ages to heal. A month or so later, I had slept in and was very gastric, no control at all. But I had an appointment for new glasses so off to town I go. When he saw me, said "I'm sending for an ambulance." I argued I was alright but as soon as my Dr. saw me, off to top floor of hospital. I don't remember the next few days under 24 hr. monitor[50]

---

[49] This is inaccurate but Grandma often had a way of recalling her own version of details. At this time I was considering studying for a doctoral degree (which I have not done) and taking a Teaching English to Speakers of Other Languages (TESOL) course in the meantime.

[50] This is the only page in Grandma's journal where the page is complete and the same story continues on the next page. It's possible Grandma added the heading on the next page as an afterthought. Given her confusion due to ill health at the time, this may explain why it begins as it does. That is, Grandma may have meant "monitoring me" but have not been well enough to record her thoughts clearly. Although Grandma refers to a "heart attack" on the next page, this is probably the result of temporary dementia resulting from a very serious infection.

Still in hopsital 2012

me, then I woke up. The resident Dr's came and fired questions and said, well her mind is okay. Apparently I had had a heart attack but I woke up. Clive was ringing me and my Dr even rang him. Later I realised that is how most of my family died. But they said because I was so fit I didn't, but it sure gave me a fright. I now have to have more help with things. Then to top the year off my good friend & neighbor up and died. I'll miss her. I listen for phone calls from my family. It is so lonely. I've started cards of a Wed again, recess now till Feb. I read a lot & play C.D's. Try and go for a walk every morning, using a walking stick. Red Cross ring me at 8 a.m. every day. Hope the new year is better. Will be 86 in February.

The new year[51] is not much better, had a few falls but at least my mind is okay. At present I have a nurse coming twice a week to dress my leg. I fell off my walker & took the skin off the shin bone. It is at last starting to heal. Can't walk though.

---

[51] This paragraph appears to have been written with a different black pen as it is lighter. It was clearly written after 2013 had begun.

Have had Clive's son Michael here last week. He is flying to China on the 16th with his studies to an orphanage for a year then when he returns he goes to Armidale UNE for his Dr'ate[52] but he wanted to see grandma before he went. I love him to bits.

My carer from Neighbor aid comes and does some shopping for me. Hopefully I'll be able to go with her next fortnight. Bushland Place deliver frozen meals once a week now & I thaw them & cook in microwave. Only main meal $4.

Don't think I'll be able to go any more outings. Intend going back to cards when I can walk. But as I said to Rohaini while my mind is okay I'm staying here.[53]

The lady opposite had a fall off her scooter, spent 2 months in rehab. I try and visit her, nobody wants to be bothered. Poor thing.

Not much on TV,[54] all repeats & I'm out of library books. It is so quiet here, no noisy neighbors. New lady in the private house next door has son & daughter at high school and a lovely Labrador dog.

---

[52] This section is a little confused. I went to China after studying TESOL to assist with the establishment of an English tutoring school. The same organisation also ran an orphanage in Thailand but I was not involved with it. I was considering taking my doctoral degree at the University of New England in Armidale but did not pursue it after returning to Australia.

[53] Grandma desired to remain in the retirement village as long as possible. However, her weakening legs (due to an infection) eventually meant that she had to move into the nursing home even though her mind was still relatively well throughout most of the day. Although her legs improved to the point where she could walk again, she remained in the nursing home thereafter.

[54] It was a common complaint in this era that television stations provided little worth watching.

Kay & I stayed at motel in Laurieton early this year.[55] *We will go somewhere when the weather is warmer. I have the air-cond. on 1 hour mourning & evening. I feel the cold. Most of the roads need fixing, land-slides on mountain. Have had an old photo printed and given to Wingham Museum as I'm the last of issue alive. The road passed the school is named Stennett Road.*[56] *One to Tinone too. I've yet to see them. Will wait untill the weather is warmer before we go again.*

Health.

Had some bad falls. The district nurses have been calling twice a week to dress my leg. Took the skin off my shin bone; spent over 4 weeks with it elevated. Nearly better. My carer takes me shopping once a fortnight. Look forward to going out. The neighbor aid bus gave me a lovely box of fruit & meat enough to last a long while. I get meals frozen from Bushland health delivered to my door. Only $4 each. So I'm well looked after.

---

[55] Based on the surrounding texts, 2013 must be intended.
[56] This road on Comboyne was named after Grandma's late father. The primary school is still located towards one end of it.

Xmas 2013

I am now a permanent resident of Bushland Hostel.[57] Clive & Rohaini and Kay & family moved me as I couldn't look after myself anymore. I use a walker all the time now though my legs are getting stronger. I am well looked after. Have a lovely room, my own TV and music & a chair which I can sit or lie down in. The bed belongs the hostel, it raises up or down. The nurses shower me every morning and I go to the dining room to have meals. They take my pension and I have some spending money left. Everyone is very good to me, and it saves my family from worry.

My doctor cut some skin things off my nose; he said he'll give me taxi vouchers later in January.

I try and go for a walk every morning to keep fit. They have games & exercises every day and I read library books. Clive got me a speaker phone which I'm still learning to use. Everyone is nice to me.

I try & go in town twice a week just to exercise my legs and when I back here I walk round the complex.

---

[57] i.e. the nursing home.

Marriages

I was married at 23 to Dennis Astle. I had two children Trevor and Clive. The marriage lasted about 16 years. Dennis' father visited the boys for Christmas each year in Taree but Dennis had very little contact with his sons.

In my 50's, I married Jack Kennedy. He was a kind gentleman. We met and romanced at Parents Without Partners, a social group for unattached parents. Jack and I liked to go ballroom dancing every week. At this time I was on my own as both sons had moved away for work.

Jack helped me create a lovely garden, a passion we shared. We loved to watch TV together, holding hands and sharing Cadbury milk chocolate that Jack would surprise me with regularly. The gifts were so frequent I asked Jack to stop as I was putting on too much weight!

I've always loved loved[58] cats. Rufus used to sleep under the house in the sun. The fox terrier strolled past one day & puss jumped on his back, boy he rode him like a jockey across the road & up the street then sat like a king on the gate post; he never came again. He lived 18 years. Next I had a ginger one. The schoolteacher left & left puss; he was jealous. I could feed their cat but he would chase theirs home.[59]

I try & go in to Taree twice a week & my legs are good, keeps my mind alert too.

I read library books & meet people I used to know. Dr keeps me in ½ price taxi. Michael has a car now & visited me.[60] I'm very proud of him. He's now got his certificate in English, been a missionary over in China. [61]He has visited me here. I've just had the service man visit me. I broke the handle on my walker, he has temporarily fixed it, will come back on Mon. I was going out in Taree. He was sick.

I'll have to be more carefull.

Rohaini's mother died,[62] she was younger than me. I'll be 88 on Feb next year 2015. They look after me well. Dr. visits me here. My sugar is under control.[63] I don't see the eye specialist till next year.

---

[58] Grandma wrote the word twice. Perhaps it was her intent to emphasise it?

[59] Although this paragraph retells a tale previously related, as it provides extra detail and highlights a prominent memory for Grandma, in addition to how this is the final page of her completed journal entries, it seemed best to retain it in spite of the repetition.

[60] I visited Grandma during my short trip back to Australia just after Chinese New Year, during their holiday period. From memory, I could not return in time for Grandma's birthday but came shortly afterwards.

[61] The ink changes to blue at this point for no apparent reason.

[62] This was on the 14th of February 2014. I had briefly seen her in hospital in Brisbane only the day before. As one might imagine, having both their mothers ailing made this a very stressful time for my father and step-mum.

[63] This refers to Grandma's need as a diabetic to regularly check her sugar levels.

Extra Stories

This is where the journal ends. However, Grandma included a list of other stories she had planned to write had her health not declined. I asked some relatives to fill in the details for a couple. They are included in the following pages.

The list presented below is a copy of Grandma's own excluding those for which additional details have been supplied.

- *Toy wheel barrow thrown by sister landed though open window at feet of visitors*

- *Danny the DJ*

- *Shopping 2 mile to grocer large suitcase*

- *Helping ourselves to mandarins.*

- *Slab of butter thrown at Doris imprint on wall-paper*

- *Picking potatoes and peas. Mum's remark about how late Bob & I were, his reply.*

- *Jody's accident*

- *Double toilet newspapers only pans.*

- *Jack's[64] scrub turkeys nest no turkeys but leeches in a plenty.*

- *I have creek eel grab my toe Bob laughed*

---

[64] This could refer to Grandma's brother Jack however it probably refers to her final husband who was also known as "Jack" (even though his name was Harry) as a result of a mistaken identity which stuck.

My first day at Chatham Primary School[65]

I was 5. I had attended Comboyne School for 6 months before moving to Taree.

My first day at Chatham school, my brother took me to school and arranged to meet me at the gate after school. During the day I had a wonderful time meeting lots of new school friends. When school ended I was talking with one of my new friends as he walked home. When we got to the school gate I didn't recognise anything and my brother was nowhere to be seen.

I continued on to my new friend's home. His parents kindly gave me dinner. I was not concerned or worried at all. His parents asked where I lived. I said I didn't know as I'd only just moved. The best I could volunteer was "near a big park." They drove me around town asking if I recognised anything. I didn't but it was fun looking. After quite some time it grew dark.

Eventually we came to the big park I recognised and there was my brother and mother searching frantically. I didn't know why they were upset as I was fine! I thought Mum would give me a belting but she never did.

---

[65] My father wrote this story based upon his own recollection of the event. Grandma's listed title for it was, "Clive lost 1st day Chatham School."

> *Walking to hospital standing all day ironing then walk home when boys were young.*[66]

After Gladys moved to Taree, life was a struggle. At the time, it was very difficult for women to find work. Jobs were preferentially given to married men to support their family. Gladys had herself and two young boys under 8 to support and no maintenance from her former husband. But society ostracised divorced women.

Gladys found work at the hospital at Taree, working in the laundry but at a pay half that of what a man would have been paid. The determined 35-year old rose in the dark and walked 5km to work, then stood all day in a very hot room with steaming irons. Gladys walked another 5km home at the close of each work day. Gladys had then to prepare dinner for the boys and the next day's lunches. There were no modern conveniences. Washing was done in a copper boiler, clothes stirred with a broom handle and dried by hand wringing through a mechanical device attached to the laundry sink. An exhausted Gladys often found herself at the end of a long day staring blankly ahead, chronically depressed and facing what seemed a hopeless future. There was no time or energy to play with her children like modern parents. Survival would have to be enough. Often there was only enough food for the boys. Gladys missed many meals despite growing her own vegetables. There was simply not enough money no matter how hard Gladys tried.

---

[66] This is the exact title Grandma listed for this story.

Index of Pictures

Me in my prime..Cover & title page
Me as a baby with a cow...5
Me on a horse...6
Jean & brother Bob's Wedding..7
Bess, Doris & Me..8
Doris & Me..9
Doris & Me in bathers...10
Me with sister May[67]...11
Grandma & Grandpa Hutchby[68] (damaged)................................12
Me with the boys...13
Me with a car..15
Me with Mum (Beatrice), May, Edna & Doris................................16
Me in a dress..17
Stennett siblings as children...18
Stennett siblings 1964 (Jack, Me, Bill, Doris, Bob, Edna, Albert, May)...........19
Beatrice with 9 children[69]..20
Me in a frock...21
Me under my mango tree..22
Me with Trevor & Clive on the porch in Mudford St......................23
John & Beatrice with Albert, Edna, Bob, & (back) Harry, Bill, Jack & May....24
Rufus by the sewing machine..25
Me on my 80th birthday..26
House[70]...27
Brother Harry on his motorbike..28
Me and Mum in Sydney...29
Me and Mum with Brother Albert in his airforce uniform.............30
Grandma[71]..31
Grandma & Grandad Stennett[72]..33
Me with Trevor, Doris (his wife), Jody & baby Haley..................34
All of us at the zoo..35
Me with Michael & Rohaini...36
Me with husband Jack...37
Me with Danny, Mika & Rio at Bushland Hostel........................43
Me on my 87th birthday..Back cover

---

[67] The other people are not labelled.
[68] Parents of Beatrice
[69] Kay thought this was taken the day of John's funeral.
[70] Nobody seems to be able to identify where this house was nor who it belonged to.
[71] I.e. the grandmother of Gladys
[72] Parents of John

Epilogue

I had intended to publish this book earlier however the widely bemoaned continuing disruptive events which began in 2020 caused significant delays. Sadly, Grandma passed away on 17th August 2021 in her room at Bushland Hostel in Taree. Perhaps most unfortunately, New South Wales was in so strict a lockdown at that time that even her niece Kaye on Comboyne had to obtain a special travel permit to collect her remains. As all of her immediate family live interstate, none of us were permitted to attend her funeral. Nonetheless, Kaye kindly ensured a recording of it was made and shared. Although Grandma's last words remain unknown to us, in her final days she was often known to say, "I've had a good life, a hard life, but a good life."

Advertising

Play Traitor Chess
by Issachar Saberhagen
(ISBN: 9780994179920)
What if there were traitors on the chessboard? What if the soldiers sometimes followed the orders of the other king? In Traitor Chess, it happens! Learn how to play with this quick guide to the basic rules and some variations.

From Sailor to Samurai:
The Legend of a Lost Englishman
by Jessy Carlisle
(ISBN: 9781922758651)
Based upon the true story of William Adams, this historical fiction forms part of the *Bilingual Legends* series for children. The text is presented in both English and Japanese.

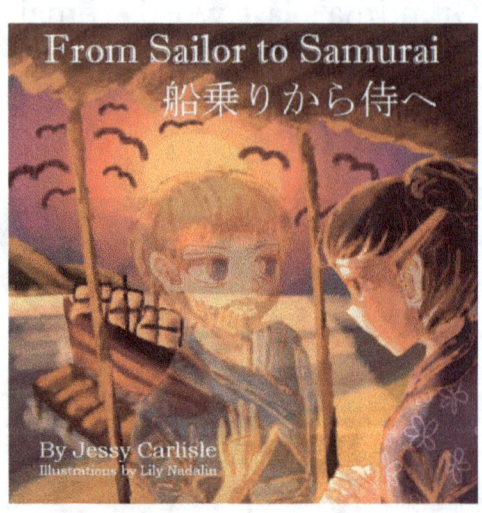

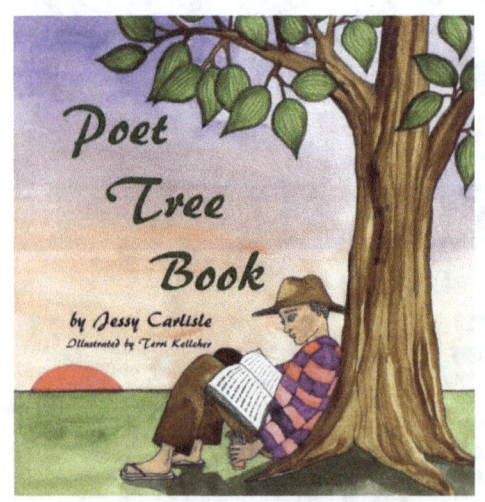

Poet Tree Book
by Jessy Carlisle
(ISBN: 9780994179913)
The author's premier publication of poems including the iconic piece "A Tree's Lament" which was first publicly performed at the Queensland Poetry Slam.

www.ingramcontent.com/pod-product-compliance
Lightning Source LLC
Chambersburg PA
CBHW080901010526
44118CB00015B/2230